Emotional Intelligence:

How to Succeed By Mastering Your Emotions And Raising Your IQ

By Michele Gilbert

<u>Visit My Amazon Author Page</u>

Dedicated to those who choose to stretch beyond their own limits and to seek a more abundant and fulfilling life.

Your thoughts are creative.

Michele Gilbert

Table of contents

Introduction

Welcome to the world of Emotional Intelligence (EI)!

Well, maybe 'welcome' isn't necessarily accurate because you've been experiencing emotions since you the day you were born.

Since day 1, you've cried, thrown fits, smiled, laughed, and loved.

Have you ever spent a day with a baby?

You'll know that they experience the whole range of emotions, and sometimes switch from extreme joy to full-blown rage in the blink of an eye.

The fact of being human is that emotions are an unavoidable, in-built part of life. We are born with this emotional system in place.

There is no way to avoid them, to ignore them, or to have them not affect your life in one way or another.

The common misconception regarding Emotional Intelligence is that it's a way to suppress your true feelings, to present yourself as happy even though you are sad, and to manipulate other people by using how they feel to your advantage.

What's interesting, however, is how suppressing feelings, misrepresenting how you really feel, and manipulating other people are actually all symptoms of a lack of Emotional Intelligence!

As David Caruso points out, "Emotional Intelligence is not the opposite of intelligence, it is not the triumph of heart over head – it is the unique intersection of both."

Think about it.

If you aren't paying attention to how you feel, then you are, by definition, suppressing and ignoring your true feelings.

If you don't know how you really feel in a situation, how can you accurately represent and communicate those emotions to someone else?

And, manipulation and deception are common traits of people who lack a sense of empathy, which is a core component of Emotional Intelligence.

Through this brief thought experiment, and throughout the rest of this short book, it will slowly dawn on you that many of your current problems, dissatisfactions, and challenges are simply the result of a lack of Emotional Intelligence.

Research in recent decades has almost unequivocally proven that Emotional Intelligence helps people in almost every facet of their lives. People who develop the core skills experience:
- A newfound sense of self regarding what's important to them and why
- Sky-rocketed levels of self-esteem
- An unprecedented amount of courage that fosters creative expression and ambition
- Better, stronger relationships
- Dramatic improvements in their effectiveness as both a leader and a teammate
- Overall higher earnings at work due to heightened levels of achievement, promotions, and higher performance ratings from superiors and peers
- An improved ability to influence and persuade others through compassion and empathy rather than coercion and selfishness

What's important to understand is that these benefits aren't all just hype. Each one is backed by *multiple* scientific, peer-reviewed studies. These studies are outlined in Chapter 2.

You see, the data indicates that the importance of EI is so strong that the question is not whether becoming more emotionally intelligent will change your life, but rather how much time and energy are you willing to invest to develop your emotional intelligence.

The question is: 'What kind of life do you believe you deserve?'

The question is: 'What quality of life are you ready to achieve?'

The question is: 'What is earning more money, improving your relationships, and actually *changing for the better* worth to you?'

The unfortunate reality is that even when people are presented with a solution to their problems, they don't actually take the time to implement the solution, unless it's a 'quick-fix' or 'magic pill.'

Why? Because the effort, discomfort, and pain associated with *changing* is typically greater than the satisfaction and comfort that a better lifestyle affords.

A 'quick-fix' implies no effort, no pain, and no time. You just do this, take this, or read this, and BAM! life is suddenly better.

However, that's marketing hype instead of real life.

So, I want to be straight with you from the beginning.

Although I can't promise a 'quick-fix' or that reading these words will transform you from the inside out, what I can promise is that if you take the time to read this short book, you will not only understand the importance of EI in your life, but also the daily habits that, when implemented, will incrementally raise your EI day-by-day.

With your courage, commitment, and conscious action, you will experience a new quality of life that conforms to your passion and purpose, rather than trying to trick yourself into believing that your current circumstances are right for you.

Imagine a life consisting of a career you're passionate about, people you care about, and the self-confidence to believe that you deserve it all, and more!

No matter where you are in your life, how old you are, or how many times you've messed up in the past, you have the power to change.

But, in order for you to experience the benefits of Emotional Intelligence, you have to do your part.

You can't expect to just read these words, gloss over the exercises, never put anything into practice, and have everything change for you.

Albert Einstein said it best when he defined insanity as "doing the same thing over and over and expecting different results."

So, here's what you need to do.

First, read this book all the way through, right now, while you're thinking about it.

It will only take you 30 minutes.

Next, and this is the most important thing, perform at least 2 of the exercises found in chapter 3 right when you read them. They are short, sweet, and seriously effective.

Then, you need to continue to perform at least 2 of the exercises *on a daily basis.*

Look, do yourself this favor: make Emotional Intelligence a priority in your life for the next 7 days. All I'm asking for is 1 week.

If you see some results and improvement, which you will, then continue for another week, then a month, then a year, then a lifetime.

But, I want to advise against the 'New Year's Resolution' type of commitment. Setting the standard for 365 days can be a daunting task.

So, instead, make it easy. Just 7 days.

The first and most important thing you can do to instill that sense of dedication to this part of your life is to turn the page.

For the next 30 minutes, open your mind to a new perspective on your life and how you can achieve all your goals with less stress.

I'm excited to show you how.

See you on the next page.

CHAPTER 1
What Emotional Intelligence REALLY Is

"Anybody can become angry. That is easy. But to be angry with the right person, and to the right degree, and at the right time, and for the right purpose, and in the right way, that is not within everybody's power and is not easy." ~Aristotle

Before we delve into concepts, ideas, and the world of your mind, I want you to pause and check in to the world of your heart.

Take a couple deep breaths. Say 'ahhhh' on the exhale.

Really pause for a moment. Allow yourself to tune into exactly what is going on inside you right now.

Ask yourself some questions:
- How am I feeling right now?
- What is the *name* or *label* of that emotion? (i.e. sadness, excitement, anxiety, etc.)
- What shade of that emotion am I feeling? (i.e. anger can range from frustrated and annoyed to infuriated and raged)
- Where in my body do I experience that feeling?
- What triggered, and continues to trigger, this emotion?

There is no right or wrong answer to these questions. But, pay attention to whether you were able to answer these questions quickly, like the answer was obvious, or whether you struggled to search for the right word for the emotion and its exact location.

If you found the exercise a little difficult, that's ok. In fact, it's completely normal.

Hopefully, this exercise will illustrate how <u>there is a sharp distinction between experiencing emotions and *intelligently* acting on them.</u>

Now, if you're one of the few who didn't immediately perform the exercise, remember when I encouraged you to do the exercises as you come across them in the book? Well, here's your first chance.

Really take one quick moment to check in with yourself right now and see how you're feeling.

EI researchers call this activity a 'Check-In' because you turn off the focus from your mind, and you *check in* with your heart and your body.

This reflective skill represents that foundation for healthy self-awareness, which is the first of four key skills that comprise EI.

In total, Emotionally Intelligent people are skilled at 4 things:
1) Self-Awareness
2) Self-Management
3) Social Awareness
4) Relationship Management

Peter Salovey and John Mayer published this conception of Emotional Intelligence as a developable skill set rather than an innate capacity in their 1990 seminal work <u>Imagination, Cognition, and Personality</u>.

To quote their definition of EI, it's "a set of skills hypothesized to contribute to the accurate appraisal and expression of emotion in oneself and in others, the effective regulation of emotion in self and others, and the use of feelings to motivate, plan and achieve in one's life." Put another way, "the emotionally intelligent individuals accurately perceive their emotions and use integrated, sophisticated approaches to regulate them as they proceed toward important goals."

Let's break down the definition a little further in order to see what each of the four skills really entails.

Self-awareness deals with the 'accurate appraisal and expression of emotion in oneself' and forms the foundation of self-confidence.

Self-management involves 'the effective regulation of emotion in self... and the use of feelings to motivate, plan and achieve in one's life.' High-EI individuals act on emotional information in an intelligent way, which psychologists Sternberg and Salter define as 'goal-directed adaptive behavior.' We will delve into this concept in the next chapter.

Social awareness transfers the capacities of self-awareness to other people. This skill is the basis of empathy and an orientation toward serving and helping others rather than serving oneself.

Similarly, relationship management involves regulating, planning with, and motivating a group of people. High-EI leaders are proficient influencers, persuaders, and collaborators. They excel at teamwork, conflict management, and motivating peers to perform at their highest levels.

Through this brief description, you can hopefully start to see how practicing these skills on daily basis will powerfully, positively, and permanently impact your life and relationships.

A Quick Thought Experiment

"When a person has access to both the intuitive, creative, and visual right brain, and the analytical, logical, verbal left brain, the whole brain is working... and this tool is best suited to the reality of what life is, because life is not just logical – it is also emotional."
~Stephen Covey

Again, for a moment, let's take a step back and work through another mental exercise.

Let's imagine that you are trying to solve a 1,000-piece jigsaw puzzle.

The catch is that you only have a vague idea about what the complete picture should look like.

How would you go about solving this puzzle?

The fact is that without the total picture, you don't know whether you have all the necessary pieces to complete the puzzle, and you could have a number of problems, such as pieces that fit for a different puzzle entirely, or not enough pieces to start with, and so on.

So, although you have all of these small jigsaw pieces with parts of a total picture on them, you can't effectively or intelligently put them together.

In real life, this same problem happens when you are faced with an emotional crisis or life decision.

Suddenly, you are bombarded with an intense *life puzzle* and an abundance of emotional information.

More than likely, you'll have mixed emotions, an unclear idea about what to do, and no useful way to determine what your intuition, emotions, and even logic are telling you to do.

Again, when trying to solve a logic puzzle with incomplete information, totally wrong ideas, or confusing terms, do you think it's possible to arrive at right answer?

Similarly, when trying to solve a life puzzle with incomplete emotional information, totally wrong ideas about the significance of those emotions, or confusing emotions, do you think it's possible to solve your own problems?

Of course not!

The Difference Between EI and IQ

One question you might be asking yourself is: if Emotional Intelligence is so important, then why is it that our culture values GPA, SAT scores, and IQ?

Shouldn't we all be emotional geniuses?

The answer is that our culture's attitude about emotions is that they are in direct opposition to logic, reason, and rationality. That it's EI vs. IQ.

Emotions 'cloud your judgment,' people get 'blinded by anger,' and business people often warn against 'becoming too emotionally involved.'

Additionally, people typically view emotions in a negative light. They focus on emotions only when they are stressed out, insecure, or experiencing a bout of rage during rush hour traffic.

On the one hand, this view acknowledges the core fact that the *experience of emotions* is separate from *Emotional Intelligence*.

On the other hand, however, this perspective negatively brands emotions and thus excludes them as a source of information in the decision making process.

According to neuroscientific studies, the parts of your brain responsible for emotion are separate from the parts of your brain responsible for intelligence.

Emotional circuitry first developed as an alarm system that would instantaneously respond to threats in a fight-or-flight fashion.

Rewinding the clock, it makes sense that evolution would favor animals that had sophisticated methods of both identifying when a noise or visual cue indicated a threat and preparing the body to either defend against or run away from that external threat.

Animals that could correctly identify and prepare against these threats would survive, while others would die out.

Once the emotional fight-or-flight emotional system evolved to a certain point of proficiency, evolution started to favor an animal's ability to discriminate between real threats and imaginary threats.

Think about how much extra energy an animal would expend if it had a full-blown anxiety attack every time a bush rustled or something fell off a tree.

The truth is that the ability to sift through all the noises and visual cues in an intelligent way only evolved very recently. If you look at the structure of the brain, the part responsible for intelligence and executive function exists as a layer above and around the part responsible for emotional reactions.

This supplementary capacity for intelligently differentiating between the real and the fake, known as 'the critical factor,' doesn't replace the emotional circuitry, but can help interrupt its ability to hijack the body.

For example, if a cabinet slams shut, you'll notice that even a lazy cat, without the critical factor, will jump up and start running away.

The typical human, however, will experience that same surge of adrenaline, but won't be so overwhelmed by it that they literally have to run away.

Again, without that 'critical factor,' the emotion will hijack and take control of your body.

The problem and twist in this story is that as intelligence evolved to a greater degree, adding 1 full pound of mass to a human adult's brain, it developed the capacity to overlook and ignore emotions.

Today, the average person can experience heightened levels of stress, anxiety, and anger on an ongoing basis without it dramatically affecting their ability to survive and function.

But, although both low- and high-EI people can survive and function, the high-EI people are much more effective in their personal, professional, and love lives.

Exactly how and why, and the data supporting these claims, are the topics of the next chapter.

Keep reading.

CHAPTER 2
Why EQ Determines A Person's Life Success

"Rule your feelings, lest your feelings rule you." ~Publilius Syrus

The reason I wrote these words and published this e-book is because I want you to experience a complete paradigm shift.

Hopefully, you will begin to view anger, sadness, guilt, embarrassment, shame, and other 'negative' emotions as vital sources of information, key indicators that you need to change something in your life.

Additionally, you will start to pay more attention to the feelings of happiness, excitement, elation, and other 'positive' emotions in order determine the underlying causes of joy in your life.

Through the exercises presented in chapter 3, you will not only immerse yourself in the world of emotions, but also start to understand exactly how you feel and why you feel that way, and what triggered, and continues to trigger, that emotion.

First Emotional Information, Then Emotional Intelligence

The basis of Emotional Intelligence, and the goal of this book, is the assertion that the emotions that you are already experiencing on a day-to-day basis, whether 'positive' or 'negative,' are brimming with relevant information regarding how you can maintain a happy, healthy, effective lifestyle.

The fact of the matter is that regardless of your current level of Emotional Intelligence, you are experiencing and being affected by emotions every day.

Emotions represent the mood you're in when you wake up...

They're how you feel about what you have to do that day, and how well you do those things...

They're both how other people see you and how you see yourself....

They're your mood as you go to sleep...

And on and on and on.

Emotions are everywhere, involved in everything, and are the foundation for most of the decisions you have made in your life and will make in the future.

Everyone would like to think that they can rise above the level of emotions and function on a purely rational, logical level.

But, we are, at our core, emotional creatures.

It's important to remember that the evolutionary timeline, and the resulting structure of our brain, illustrates that we were first emotional, unintelligent creatures.

Emotions developed before intelligence.

We now have both emotions *and* intelligence. Again, we have both EI and IQ.

But, they are not the two opposing forces, as culture would have you believe.

Instead, as Jensen, Rideout, Freedman & Freedman explain, the benefit of intelligence is that we now have "a way of recognizing, understanding, and choosing how we think, feel and act."

In fact, the study that this quote comes from goes on to conclude that "research suggest [EI] is responsible for as much as 80% of the 'success' in our lives."

The Research

1) EI Boosts IQ

A 2002 study found, with over 99% confidence that students with high-EI will score higher on cognitive tests than students with low-EI. Their concluding paragraph asserted many reasons for the marked difference.

First, they reasoned that the high-EI individuals were better at managing their emotional state, reducing stress, and staying more focused on the test during the allotted time. Thus, although two students could have similar cognitive abilities, the high-EI participant would have a clear advantage.

Second, they argued that whereas naturally high-EI was typically associated with higher-IQ, a person with low-EI could either have high- or low-IQ. In other words, high-EI individuals are almost always smart, and low-EI individuals can be just as smart, but still score worse on the tests.

2) Employers hire high-EI applicants

In 2012, the Department of Labor studied a variety of companies in order to answer the central question: 'What are today's companies looking for in new hires?'

Through reductive analysis, they were able to boil down the answers to 7 simple responses. Their shocking finding was that out of these 7 qualities, the first 6 (the ones most sought after) all correlate to high levels of Emotional Intelligence.

Qualities such as 'collaboration skills,' 'ability to take initiative,' and 'self-confidence,' ended up at the top of the list. At the bottom, the only non-EI attribute, was 'math and reading abilities,' which represents an obvious minimum requirement.

Another national study found that 2 out of 3 companies rank high-EI as the most important attribute for new hires. At the highest level, 100%, 3 out of 3, of the Fortune 500 and 100 companies prioritized high-EI.

3) At work, EI beats IQ and technical knowledge

Further research distilled on-the-job competency into three domains of ability: cognitive IQ, technical expertise, and Emotional Intelligence scores. The investigation found that Emotional Intelligence is twice as powerful as both IQ and technical expertise *combined*.

4) High-EI representatives enhance customer satisfaction

Many studies performed over a range of professions, from health-care physicians and teachers to sales representatives and waiters, all consistently demonstrate that clients and customers of high-EI representatives and caretakers self-report higher levels of satisfaction with both the business and the representative.

5) High-EI individuals are better at coping with and managing stress

In 2003, a group of researchers discovered that Emotional Intelligence was inversely proportional to levels of both perceived and experienced stress. In other words, students with higher EI scores were not only more adept at dealing with stressful situations as they arose, but also evaluated situations as overall less stressful than their low-EI counterparts.

6) High-EI individuals are better at coping with and managing anger

Through cross-cultural studies of anger management participants, many studies have consistently demonstrated both that the classes raise EI levels and that these higher levels of EI assist people in dealing with and managing anger.

One interesting commonality in these studies' findings was the overarching character change that results from heightened EI. Aggressiveness turns into assertiveness, a bossy person becomes strong-willed, demanding individuals simply become ambitious, and confrontational people end up being decisive.

7) High-EI individuals make more effective leaders

A host of studies performed at the turn of the century found that high-EI workers have a transformational impact on their peers and overall working environment.

Through the intelligent use of emotions, leaders and managers improve interpersonal relationships between co-workers, improving trust, cooperation, and decision making processes.

The expression of positive emotions and optimism creates a vision for a better future and instills a sense of enthusiasm within the ranks.

Also, peers consistently view high-EI individuals, even subordinates, as happier, more committed to the organization, and a better employee than their smart, but low-EI, co-workers.

8) EI correlates with job satisfaction

From 2008-2009, researchers tracked and analyzed 215 teachers. Through even casual testing, they found significant positive relationships between each component of Emotional Intelligence that they measured and a teacher's skills, motivation, and job satisfaction.

Higher-EI scores correlated with improvements in each of these key areas!

9) EI correlates with satisfaction in romantic relationships

A 2011 meta-analysis, reviewing the results of 6 previously completed studies, found a "significant correlation between trait emotional intelligence and romantic relationship satisfaction." In fact, they discovered that higher levels of EI improved the satisfaction of both parties, even if the spouse had low-EI.

Thus, taking the time to enhance your Emotional Intelligence could improve your relationship with your significant other!

Although the list goes on and on, the most important takeaway from the body of research done on EI is

10) EI is a teachable and learnable skill

There are so many studies that demonstrate, beyond a shadow of doubt, that reading about EI, taking classes, and performing certain exercises, like the one's provided in the next chapter, can improve your EI.

One 2003 study of graduate students in particular provided some pretty staggering results.

The researchers separated participants into 5 classes. While 4 of these classes taught a curriculum without Emotional Intelligence, 1 included formal instruction on Emotional Intelligence.

At the end of the course curriculum, students in the EI-curriculum group improved their scores by 8.5 more points on average than the non-EI group. That's almost a full letter grade difference.

As stated in the introduction of this book, 'the data indicates that the importance of EI is so strong that the question is not whether becoming more emotionally intelligent will change your life, but rather how much time and energy are you willing to invest to develop your emotional intelligence.'

So, if I provided you with some short, simple, and seriously effective exercises, would you perform at least two of them on a daily basis?

How much is being smarter, receiving promotions, effectively managing stress and anger, being a better leader, and liking your job and relationships more worth to you?

I have great news for you if you said anything more than 20 minutes of your time on a daily basis, because that's all it takes to follow the exercise regimen laid out in the next chapter.

CHAPTER 3
Top Keys to Develop Your Emotional Intelligence

"Emotional Intelligence is a different way of being smart. It includes knowing what your feelings are and using your feelings to make good decisions in life. It's being able to manage distressing moods well and control impulses. It's being motivated and remaining hopeful and optimistic when you have setbacks in working toward goals. It's empathy; knowing what the people around you are feeling. And it's social skill – getting along well with other people, managing emotions in relationships, being able to persuade or lead others." ~Daniel Goleman

Developing your Emotional Intelligence boils down to improving your abilities in four key areas:
- Self-awareness
- Self-management
- Social awareness
- Relationship management

As you can see, half of these skills involve 'Awareness' of what is already occurring, and the other half involves 'Management' of either yourself or others.

A common misconception about Emotional Intelligence is that women naturally have more than men. But, research into this rumor has found it to be false.

Whereas women naturally score higher on the self- and social-awareness skills, men without training score higher on the self- and relationship-management skills.

When analyzing all the skills as a composite score, however, women and men maintain similar averages.

Thus, don't let your age, gender, or perceived lack of Emotional Intelligence stop you from moving forward and performing these practices on a daily basis.

Once again, I want to stress that if you find one or two exercises that appeal to you, I want you to immediately stop reading and preform the exercise right then, before you go any further.

Then, I want you to continue performing that exercise on a daily basis for the next 7 days. Keep only the next 7 days in your mind during this period of training.

The Exercises

EI Skill #1: Self-Awareness

1) 'Check-In'

a. At any point in your day, close your eyes and take a couple of deep breaths. Say 'ahhh' on the exhale unless you're in public.

b. Tune into your body. Feel your feet on the ground if you are standing or sitting.

c. Scan your body for tension. When you find a tense area, remain aware of it without trying to immediately change it.

d. Ask yourself

    i. What would I label this feeling?

    ii. What shade of that feeling would I call this tension?

    iii. What triggered, and continues to trigger this feeling?

e. Notice any thoughts, memories, or other feelings arising as you examine this emotion more closely.

f. Continue breathing and following the tension until you have a clear label for the emotion and what is causing it.

g. Solidify in your mind what you are going to write down before you open your eyes.

h. Write down your emotions along with a time stamp, a note of where you were, and some context about what you were just doing and about to do.

2) Journal

a. At the end of your day, record the most emotionally powerful events. Make sure to write down both positively and negatively powerful moments. It helps if you perform check-ins during these moments during the day and have the time stamp and context already written down.

b. If you haven't performed a check-in, close your eyes and reflect on that moment. Mentally place yourself in that same situation and ask yourself the questions as if you were performing a check-in in that moment.

c. Ask yourself some additional questions

    i. Does this emotion, and how I react, represent a pattern in my behavior?

1. When does this pattern typically arise?

2. How often do I experience this pattern?

ii. Would I want to duplicate my behavior in the future?

1. If not, what's a better way for me to behave when caught in this pattern?

iii. How did other people react to my behavior?

EI Skill #2: Self-Management

1) Write yourself notes or phone alerts from what you've discovered during your journaling and check-in sessions in order to avoid repeating negative behavior patterns.

2) Actively pause, when you catch yourself getting swept up by an emotion. You don't need to perform an entire check-in, but engage your mind and think about what is going on.

a. Ask yourself whether there is another way to describe the situation you *think* you are trapped in.

b. Create a new perspective by interpreting and describing the situation in an entirely different way, from a unique point of view.

3) During an emotional dialogue, pause and find an honest, clear expression of your feelings.

a. Psychologists typically suggest 'I' statements that involve the form of 'I feel _____, when you do _____.'

4) Mentally, or with your journal, revisit the situation later to discover your triggers and your patterns of behavior. Through experience, you will learn your strengths, weaknesses, and 'hot buttons.'

a. Compile a list of your 'hot buttons' and carry them around with you. Familiarize yourself with that list in order to catch your emotional circuitry hijacking you in the moment.

EI Skills #3: Social Awareness

1) Journal

a. In these entries, focus on how other people were feeling and what you noticed about their expressions.

    i. Ask whether their emotions represented patterns of behavior for them.

    ii. Try to determine their triggers, especially if you caused the emotional moment.

    iii. Write out strategies for both how you can avoid triggering that emotional moment in the future and how you would prefer to act if that same situation were to arise in the future.

b. Focus on the similarities between what you've noticed about yourself and other people. Typically, triggers and patterns that apply to you will be the same for others. We are all human, after all.

2) Pay attention to other people during conversations and throughout your day. Take the focus off of yourself from time to time not only to clear your head, but also to take the 'emotional temperature' of the environment around you. Especially at work, it can help your reputation to notice when someone is unhappy, so that you can cheer them up.

3) Rather than asking people 'how are you?' ask them 'how happy are you on a scale of 1-10?' You are sure to get juicy answers if you're genuinely interested and have the time to listen.

4) "Seek first to understand, then to be understood." ~Steven Covey. I borrowed this habit from Covey's '7 Habits of Highly Effective People' because of how powerful it can be in the process of developing your Emotional Intelligence. When talking to other people, start focusing more on their point of view and what they are trying to express rather than getting your point across and having them agree with you.

EI Skill #4: Relationship Management

1) Let yourself be vulnerable. The goal of this exercise is to express how you feel about work, about a relationship, about insecurity, or about anything in an honest, clear fashion. Open up to somebody else, even if it's a topic entirely unrelated to them, about how you feel. Doing this on a consistent basis will help you get pent up emotions off your chest, and it will improve the quality of your relationships.

2) Think win/win/win. When making decisions, consider how it will affect you, the other person, and your relationship. You want to make sure that everyone, and the relationship, benefits from your daily choices.

3) Journal. I hope you see the consistent theme that every skill will benefit from your journaling efforts. Take the time to note what your partner or friends like, dislike, and what they are looking forward to. Note their birthdays, their anniversary dates, and other important dates for their families.

    a. To add a personal touch, you can send a card during one of these important dates.

Conclusion

Thank you, and thank yourself, for taking the time to read this short book and apply some of the life-changing exercises included herein.

By reading these words, you have demonstrated to your conscious and unconscious minds that developing Emotional Intelligence is a priority in your life.

You have taken the first step toward your new quality of life, based on compassion, empathy, emotions, and intelligence, rather than using your intelligence only to serve yourself.

The next steps involve making daily habits out of the exercises listed in the previous chapter in order to enhance the 4 core skills that comprise Emotional Intelligence.

Like I said in the introduction, there is no 'quick fix' or 'magic pill' that can help you develop Emotional Intelligence. But, it's also not a lot of hard work to get you where you want to be.

The first part of the process, and half of what makes a person Emotionally Intelligent, is simple day-to-day awareness of yourself, your behavior, and other people.

Replace all the thoughts, worries, and distractions that flood your head every minute with an awareness of your body, your mood, and how other people are feeling, as well.

Once you're performing Check-Ins on a regular basis and become more attuned to your flowing emotional states, the skills of self- and relationship-management are the next steps.

You use the knowledge you've gained from observing yourself and other people to better understand the current situation and achieve the objectives you've laid out for yourself either mentally or in your journal beforehand.

As you can see, Emotional Intelligence involves identifying the emotional patterns in yourself and others, so that you can overcome the ones that no longer serve you and tap into the ones that propel you forward.

Hopefully, the research presented in chapter 2 has removed all the doubts in your mind about whether the pursuit of higher EI is worth your time.

Before you go, I'd like to say thank you for purchasing my book.

I know you could have picked so many other books to read on understanding emotional intelligence. But you took a chance on me.

So A Big thanks for downloading this book and reading it all the way to completion.

Now I would like to ask a _small_ favor.

Could you please take a minute or two to leave a review for this book on Amazon?

Click here

The feedback will help me continue to publish more kindle books that will help people to get better results in their lives.

And if you found it helpful in anyway then please let me know :-)

Thank you and good luck!

To your success,

Michele

Preview of My New Book

The Introvert's Advantage: The Introverts Guide To Succeeding In An Extrovert World

So What Is An Introvert Anyway

The main difference between introverts and extroverts is not in their public behavior, but in the way they recharge their batteries. Introverts need a lot of alone time, but when they do strut their stuff they can do it as well as any extrovert.

You may have assumed the shy quiet person in the corner is an introvert, but that the one in the middle of the room making all the noise is definitely an extrovert. Actually, they may both be introverts. People genuinely don't always know themselves that they have an introvert personality type!

Check the chapter on Introverts versus Extroverts, but if you listen when you are told things, prefer small groups to large parties, and relax with a book or watching a favorite film, you are an introvert. Congratulations! Introverts dominate the gifted section of the community. It is far easier to learn social confidence than to learn how to cope without the restless need for constant stimulation.

The Common Misconceptions Of Introverts

The most common misconception is that all introverts have social anxieties. Actually, both introverts and extroverts may have social anxieties. We just cope with them differently. They certainly aren't a defining factor.

Contrary to what most people think, a shy person is certainly an introvert, but not all introverts are shy.

Neither do we find it difficult to have conversations. We just find small talk pointless. Interesting conversations about ideas and concepts? Now you're talking.

This leads to another misconception, that we are awkward and rude. An introvert trying to shake off a relentless extrovert may eventually have to be rude. That is something you can work on, because they don't like it!

Here are some other common misconceptions:

Introversion is a personality disorder. No, to be introvert (or extrovert) is a personality type, not a disorder. Extremes of both types are discussed in the next chapter.

Introverts don't like people. We do. We like our friends very much indeed. We just don't consider every stranger a friend we don't yet know.

Introverts don't go out in public. We do. Public is fine. If there's a point to it.

Introverts prefer to be alone. No, not *prefer*. But being alone is how we recharge. And we don't like being with people just for the sake of being with people.

Introverts don't know how to relax and have fun. Are you kidding? We just don't need to be making a noise or in the middle of a crowd to be having fun. We can do that, and enjoy it, but we don't need it.

Introverts can become extroverts. No, we can't. We can learn to be extroverted in public, but we can't become extroverts. On the other hand, we are thinkers, makers, doers, and we can be performers. Why would we want to change that?

Introvert versus Extrovert

There's a temptation to be rude about extroverts because they're unlikely ever to read this book. They're not big readers. However, this is not, nor should ever be, a case of Them versus Us. Apart from anything else, there are very few pure extroverts and introverts. Most of us combine traits of both. A few are so equally balanced they are called ambiverts; comfortable with groups and social interaction, but also relishing time alone, away from a crowd.

Click Here To Check Out The Rest of

The Introverts Guide To Succeeding In An Extrovert World

P.S. You'll find many more books like this and others under my name Michele Gilbert.

Don't miss them… here is a short list.

Stop Playing Mind Games: How To Free Yourself Of Controlling And Manipulating Relationships

Instant Charisma: A Quick And Easy Guide To Talk, Impress, And Make Anyone Like You

Chakras: Understanding The 7 Main Chakras For Beginners: The Ultimate Guide To Chakra Mindfulness, Balance and Healing

Practicing Mindfulness: Living in the moment through Meditation: Everyday Habits and Rituals to help you achieve inner peace

Michele Gilbert was born and raised in Brooklyn, New York. Drawn to literature and writing at a young age, she enrolled at Brooklyn College and majored in English. After graduation Michele did not begin writing immediately, instead she embarked on a career in the finance industry and spent the next thirty years on Wall Street.

Serendipity struck when she least expected it. After ending a long-term relationship, Michele found herself lost and unsure what the future held. She began to read books on grief and loss, looking for answers. Those led her to delve deeper into the Law of Attraction and its power. What resulted was remarkable. Not only had she begun to heal, she had also rekindled her former love of writing and discovered her life's purpose.

The years have taken her through many twists and turns, but she learned valuable lessons along the way. Today she publishes books-mostly self-help and metaphysical in nature-and feels compelled to share her knowledge with those facing similar experiences. Her greatest hope is to inspire others and show them ways to overcome adversity and gracefully accept life's inevitable low points.

Going forward, she plans to incorporate more teachings of self-help, finance and meditation. Regular meditation is very beneficial to her progress as she forges a new life. Morning rituals and positive incantations are other practices Michele embraces; they are very restorative in daily life.

As an avid hiker, Michele and fellow club members often hike the picturesque Jersey Pine Barrens. She is a history buff, voracious reader, baseball fanatic and a foodie. She also proudly supports Trout Unlimited-a national non-profit organization dedicated to conserving, protecting and restoring North America's Coldwater fisheries and their watersheds.

Michele currently resides forty minutes from Atlantic City and the Jersey Shore. She makes her home with a Blue Russian rescue cat named Jersey, though she isn't exactly sure who rescued who.

Michele really enjoys publishing books that can make a difference in people's lives. If you have any suggestions or would like to have a specific topic covered in a future book, please send an email to michelegilbertbooks@gmail.com and we will get back to you.

Thanks for reading!

www.ingramcontent.com/pod-product-compliance
Lightning Source LLC
Chambersburg PA
CBHW050924290526
45792CB00002B/867